We Like Kindergarten

By CLARA CASSIDY

Pictures by ELOISE WILKIN

A GOLDEN BOOK • NEW YORK
Western Publishing Company, Inc., Racine, Wisconsin 53404

My name is Carol.
I am going to kindergarten.
I go to kindergarten every day.

Laurie and Teddy Bear want to go
to kindergarten, too.
So does Rusty.
So does Patches.

At kindergarten I hang up
my spotted coat.
Stephen hangs up his brown coat.

All the boys and girls go into
the kindergarten.
Miss Hall is our teacher.
She plays the piano.
We sing, "Good morning to you."

Michael feeds our fish.
Susan feeds our turtles.
We take turns.
Someday it will be my turn
to feed them.

We do finger-painting.
I am painting with blue.
Karen is painting with red.

We make animals of clay.
I am making a dog.
Douglas is making an elephant.

We play games.

We play "Farmer in the Dell."

We play music.
Jack plays a drum.
Sally plays the bells.
We like to play music.

We listen while Miss Hall tells us
stories.
We sit quietly.
We like to hear stories.

We show and tell about things that happen. Mark told about his new baby sister.

Eric showed us his pet hamster.

We go outside to play.
I like to swing.
We all take turns.

We have milk to drink.
Jackie did not drink all
of his milk.

We rest on our rugs.
My rug is blue.
Tim's rug is blue, too.

We dance.
Martha and Annette dance.
Paul and Jack dance.

We like to dance.

We draw pictures.
Miss Hall hangs our pictures
on the wall.
I drew our house.
I drew a picture of Laurie
by our house.

Now it's time to say goodbye.
"Goodbye, Miss Hall.
See you tomorrow."

Laurie is waiting for me
when I come home.
So is Rusty.
So is Patches.
And so is Teddy Bear.

Now I am the kindergarten teacher.
I am Miss Carol.
Laurie and Rusty and Patches are
my boys and girls.
I play the piano. The children sing
"Good morning to you." Rusty and Patches
and Teddy Bear sing softly.
Laurie sings loudly. She is glad to
be in kindergarten.